DISCARD

EROSION AND SEDIMENTS

STEVE WILSON

PowerKiDS press™

NEW YORK

Published in 2017 by The Rosen Publishing Group, Inc.
29 East 21st Street, New York, NY 10010

Editor: Theresa Morlock
Book Design: Michael Flynn
Interior Layout: Tanya Dellaccio

Photo Credits: Cover Barna Tanko/Shutterstock.com; back cover Pitju/Shutterstock.com;
p. 4 Martin M303/Shutterstock.com; p. 5 Darwin Wiggett/Getty Images; p. 5 (inset) https://
commons.wikimedia.org/wiki/File:Niagara_Falls_(Horseshoe_Falls),_Niagara_Falls,_N.Y.,_U.S.A.,_by_
Keystone_View_Company.jpg; p. 6 Melodia plus photos/Shutterstock.com; p. 7 https://commons.wikimedia.org/
wiki/File:Oso_Mudslide_29_March_2014_aerial_view_3.jpg; p. 8 Charles Chusseau-Flaviens/ullstein bild/
Getty Images; p. 9 Enrique Aguirre/Getty Images; pp. 10, 11 https://commons.wikimedia.org/wiki/File:Baltoro_
glacier_from_air.jpg; p. 12 ronnybas/Shutterstock.com; p. 13 Gerhard Strydom/Shutterstock.com; p. 15 kampee
patisena/Getty Images; p. 16 Efimova Anna/Shutterstock.com; p. 17 Sigur/Shutterstock.com; p. 19 Gregory Rec/
Portland Press Herald/Getty Images; p. 20 https://meta.wikimedia.org/wiki/File:Dust_bowl,_Texas_Panhandle,_
TX_fsa.8b27276_edit.jpg; p. 21 Chalwat Srijankul/Shutterstock.com; p. 22 ThamKC/Shutterstock.com.

Library of Congress Cataloging-in-Publication Data

Names: Wilson, Steve.
Title: Erosion and sediments / Steve Wilson.
Description: New York : PowerKids Press, 2017. | Series: Spotlight on ecology and life science | Includes index.
Identifiers: ISBN 9781499425093 (pbk.) | ISBN 9781499426175 (library bound) | ISBN 9781499425109 (6 pack)
Subjects: LCSH: Erosion--Juvenile literature. | Sedimentary rocks--Juvenile literature. | Geochemical cycles--Juvenile
literature.
Classification: LCC QE571.W55 2017 | DDC 551.3'02--d23

Manufactured in China

CPSIA Compliance Information: Batch #BW17PK For further information contact Rosen Publishing, New York, New York at 1-800-237-9932.

CONTENTS

CHAPTER ONE

WEARING AWAY

Earth's forces are constantly shaping and reshaping the landscape around us. Over time, tall mountains are reduced to pebbles, rivers change their course, and rocky cliffs are transformed into beautiful sandy beaches. All these events are examples of erosion.

While Earth may seem huge and solid, its surface is actually very changeable. Water, wind, and ice can wear away at Earth's features. Erosion has shaped Earth's notable landforms, including the Grand Canyon and Niagara Falls.

Erosion also creates sediments, which are the tiny pieces of Earth's surface that get worn away. Wind and water carry sediments away from their starting places and **deposit** them in new places, creating new landforms. This process is part of Earth's rock cycle, a series of changes through which Earth's matter is used and reused.

GRAND CANYON

This is Horseshoe Falls, Niagara Falls, as it appeared in 2005.

Shown here is Horseshoe Falls as it appeared in the late 1800s.

5

CHAPTER TWO

MOVING WATER

Water is Earth's most effective form of erosion. Earth's water is in a constant state of motion. As part of the water cycle, water forms clouds, turns to rainfall, fills Earth's rivers, lakes, and oceans, and turns into a gas. Then the cycle starts all over again. This movement of water results in erosion.

When rain falls from the sky, raindrops can loosen and even move soil. Constant dripping can shape rocks over many years. Runoff is another common way that water

Over time, the constant rush of water smooths the surface of rocks in a river, breaking pieces off and carrying them away.

Rain can seep into and soak soil. On hills and mountains, this can result in landslides and mudslides, which are extreme forms of erosion that can be very dangerous for people.

erodes the land. New rain and melting snow create **rivulets** that carve channels into soil and stone. These channels grow in size the longer water flows through them.

Along coastal areas, the constant **tides** hammering against the shore wear away much of the land. Wave after wave, Earth's oceans wear rocks, even solid bedrock, into smaller and smaller pieces. Eventually, this process creates sandy beaches.

Have you ever stood in a stream or creek and noticed the path the water takes? Water splashes over rocks and down waterfalls and speeds around bends. This relentless motion carves new paths in the land. Over many years, rivers and streams can take new paths and even leave dry riverbeds behind. They can also wear large rocks down to tiny pebbles and sediments.

Snowmelt and too much rainfall can cause streams and rivers to overflow, causing floods. Floods are dangerous because water can flow into areas that aren't meant to be covered in water, such as highways, farms, and yards. Rushing floodwaters are a serious danger to people, animals, and **habitats**. Floods can quickly erode the land and wear away at highways and other public locations.

King Alfonso XIII of Spain is shown stuck in his carriage during a flood in Seville, Spain, in 1912.

Erosion caused by rivers and streams is called **fluvial** erosion.

CHAPTER THREE

ICE AND GLACIERS

Water can flow into tiny spaces, such as cracks in rocks. When the weather turns cold, the water that has seeped into these rocks freezes and expands, or takes up more space. This causes pressure inside rocks and breaks them apart. Over the years, the process of freezing and thawing can break rocks down into pebbles and sand.

The areas around Earth's poles are cold all year. Some places close to the poles have been covered with snow and

ice for thousands of years. As you move farther away from the poles, snow and ice may melt in the warmer months and **accumulate** again in cold months. This process also causes erosion. Glaciers are giant masses of ice that form near the poles and in colder areas, including higher **elevations**. As glaciers grow and shrink, they erode the land and create new landforms.

Glaciers flow like water, but they move much, much slower. This slow, grinding movement creates many types of landforms, including valleys, lakes, and **moraines**.

CHAPTER FOUR

WIND POWER

Water has been shaping and reshaping the planet's surface for millions of years, but it isn't the only force wearing away Earth's land. Wind also causes erosion. Years of moving air can create some very beautiful landforms.

A drought is a period when little or no rain falls in an area. Droughts make the soil very loose and can make wind erosion much worse. Droughts can also lead to dust storms.

Much like water erosion, wind erosion breaks the earth down and moves it to new places. Wind picks up light particles such as dust, soil, and sand. These small particles can wear away the land. This is called abrasion.

Wind erosion can cause major problems for people, especially farmers who live in flat, dry areas with few trees to block the wind. Wind constantly erodes shorelines as well. The sand that blows away builds up in new locations and sometimes needs to be moved to keep our beaches sandy.

CHAPTER FIVE

BREAK IT DOWN

Erosion reduces larger landforms and rocks to smaller pieces. These pieces include sediments such as pebbles, gravel, clay, silt, sand, and dust. Sediments can also contain **organic** material as well as harmful chemicals from human activities. Sediment is created and carried away by wind, water, and even glaciers.

Anywhere you find water, you will also find erosion. Swiftly moving rivers and streams carry a lot of sediment. Crashing waves reduce rocks to sand. Even raindrops can loosen soil and break rocks over time.

There are three main forms of wind sedimentation. Suspension is when very tiny particles are carried away by the wind. During saltation, medium-sized particles drift close to the ground. These particles speed up and hit the ground, which erodes more small particles. Creep describes when the wind pushes larger particles along the ground.

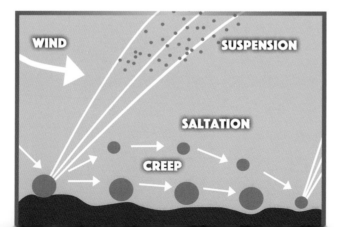

Wind has eroded the sandstone in this landscape in Thailand.

CHAPTER SIX

BUILD IT UP

Sediment that is **transported** by wind or water is eventually deposited somewhere. This could be a few feet or thousands of miles away. River sediment often comes to rest near the river's mouth. This causes new land to build up over time. This new land is called a delta.

Over the course of many years, layers of sediment build up wherever they are deposited. The weight of all the layers squeezes the sediments and turns them into rocks called

The Okavango Delta in Botswana, Africa, was formed from sediment deposited by the Okavango River.

Sediments collect at the bottom of cliffs, on beaches, on lake beds, and in many other places.

sedimentary rocks. Sedimentary rocks include sandstone, limestone, and shale. These rocks are often brittle and may break into pieces and thinner layers.

Sedimentation can have both positive and negative effects for people. River sediments that build up make new land that is good for farming. Reservoirs, or man-made lakes, fill up with sediments over time. This means there is less room for the water.

CHAPTER SEVEN

SEDIMENT STUDY

Studying sedimentation and sediment transport is very important. Geologists study sediments to understand Earth's past and how Earth's forces shape the land. Geomorphology is a science that deals with how Earth's landforms came to be. Understanding sediments and sediment transport is a large part of this science. Fluvial geomorphologists study rivers and how they erode the land and transport and deposit sediments.

Civil engineers need to understand sediments when building new structures and roads. Development projects create sediments that can blow away in the wind or be washed down nearby rivers and streams. This can include dangerous particles and pollutants, which can affect people, animals, and natural habitats.

Environmental engineers study ways to protect people from the effects of natural events, from regular rainfall to destructive hurricanes. These professionals study sediments and sediment transport to keep people and property safe.

Environmental engineers may collect samples of river water to study the sediments floating in it.

CHAPTER EIGHT

MAN-MADE EROSION

Erosion is a never-ending natural force. However, people can cause erosion to occur as well. Man-made erosion is often the result of construction and farming techniques, and it can result in many problems for people.

During the 1930s, famers in parts of Texas, Oklahoma, Kansas, Colorado, and New Mexico experienced a terrible event that earned the region the nickname the "dust bowl." In the years leading up to the 1930s, American farmers plowed up fields of grass in order to plant wheat. Without grass roots to hold the soil in place, the wind easily blew it away. A drought that lasted from 1934 to 1937 made conditions even worse. The result was giant dust clouds and failing farms.

Eroded soil forms heavy black clouds as the wind blows over this road in Texas in 1936.

LANDSLIDE

Wind and water are powerful erosive forces.

Other human activities can cause erosion.
Deforestation can cause soil erosion. It can also cause
landslides in places where they wouldn't normally happen.

CHAPTER NINE

HALTING EROSION

In some places, the natural landscape helps block erosion. Forests, hills, and mountains block wind from blowing. Natural plant cover keeps soil from blowing or washing away. When people change these natural locations, erosion can speed up. In turn, this leads to soil loss, pollution, and many other problems.

One of the easiest ways to stop erosion is to plant trees, grasses, and other plants. The roots help keep the soil in place. A modern method for reducing erosion is by using erosion control blankets. These blankets are mostly **biodegradable**, so they won't harm the soil. They were created to form a protective layer much like the layer of roots that keeps erosion from happening. Erosion control blankets also help native plants grow, and these plants then take over the job of halting erosion. Can you think of other ways to stop erosion?

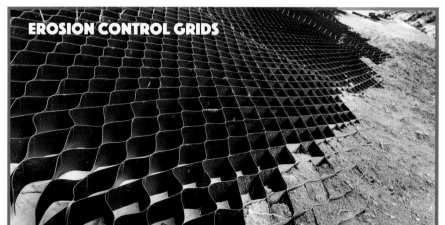

EROSION CONTROL GRIDS

GLOSSARY

accumulate (uh-KYOO-myuh-late) To gather or build up.

biodegradable (by-oh-dih-GRAY-duh-buhl) Able to be broken down naturally.

deforestation (dee-for-es-TAY-shun) Cutting down trees and clearing forested land.

deposit (dih-PAH-zuht) To put down or unload.

elevation (el-uh-VAY-shun) Height above sea level.

fluvial (FLOO-vee-uhl) Of, related to, or found in a river.

habitat (HAA-buh-tat) The natural home for plants, animals, and other living things.

moraine (muh-RAYN) Landmass formed by soil and rock deposited by a glacier.

organic (ohr-GAN-nik) Of, related to, or coming from living organisms.

rivulet (RIH-vyuh-let) A small stream of water.

tide (TYD) The rise and fall of the ocean water.

transport (tranz-PORT) To carry something from one place to another.

INDEX

PRIMARY SOURCE LIST

Page 5
Niagara Falls (Horseshoe Falls), Niagara Falls, NY, USA. Stereoscopic photograph. By Keystone View Company. Late 19th century. Now kept at the New York Public Library photography collection.

Page 8
King Alfonso XIII of Spain, and others shown during flooding in Seville, Spain. Photograph. Created by Charles Chusseau-Flaviens. Published by *Berliner Illustrirte Zeitung*. 1912.

Page 21
Heavy black clouds of dust shown over Texas Panhandle, Texas. Photograph. Created by Arthur Rothstein. 1936. Now kept at the Library of Congress, Prints and Photographs Division, Washington, D.C.

WEBSITES

Due to the changing nature of Internet links, PowerKids Press has developed an online list of websites related to the subject of this book. This site is updated regularly. Please use this link to access the list: www.powerkidslinks.com/soes/ersed